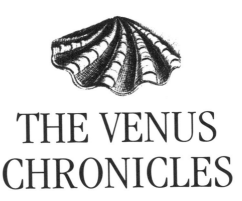

THE VENUS CHRONICLES

Musings From the Feminine Side

THE VENUS CHRONICLES

Musings From the Feminine Side

BY CAROL GEE

InnerLight Publishing • Atlanta, Georgia

Published by:

InnerLight Publishing
P.O. Box 57143
Atlanta, Georgia 30343

Cover design by Kamela Eaton
Book design by Designs by Stacey
Printed in the United States of America on acid-free paper.

Library of Congress Cataloging-in-Publication Data

LCCN 2001097025

Gee, Carol L.
    The Venus Chronicles: Musings from the Feminine Side. — 1st ed.

    ISBN 0-9714890-2-5
    I. Gee, Carol. II. Title.

10   9   8   7   6   5   4   3   2   1

This book is dedicated first to God for giving me the strength and courage to attempt this endeavor. It is dedicated to my mother, long deceased, and to my father still living. It is dedicated to Ronnie, my husband and soul mate; to my sister, Barbara, and her son, Michael, who, no matter how old he gets, will always be "our baby."

And it is dedicated to women everywhere who are experiencing life from the feminine side.

Acknowledgments

I wish to offer my thanks and gratitude to the following people:

Yolanda Johnson, Esq., my "god-daughter," for her contribution to this project. A beautiful young woman, inside and out, she listened to my zany ideas yet never once called me crazy. Her sense of humor, and the many wonderful hours we spent sharing "girl talk," as my husband called it, were catalysts for this book.

My "daughters and sons"—a small group of fine young people who call me "Mother."

My "sisters" at Emory, my faithful fan club.

My guardian angels, Joyce, Jane and Marcia.

Marymal, one of my "sheroes."

Mardi, Jala, Yolita, Evern, Michele and the two Marys of Mardi's Beauty Shop.

The women of Paradise Book Club.

Kelley and Valerie of Innerlight Publishing, for taking a chance on an unknown.

Iyanla Vanzant, for her inspiration and encouragement. Her powerful words, "Don't give up five minutes before the miracle," have become my mantra for daily life. Bernadette Griggs, personal assistant to Iyanla, whose loving hands penned the note and supplied me with lists of agents to support my journey to share the written word.

A Woman's Place

Nothing But a Number

As my 50th birthday loomed just over the horizon, I made a life-altering decision. Instead of obsessing over my uniquely female foibles, I would embrace them, maybe even write about them. Over the past half-century, I have had many life experiences that have made me less than happy I was born a woman.

Take, for example, the days when I leave for work with every strand of hair in place, looking like a middle-aged poster child for beauty on a budget, only to reach my destination looking like someone who has endured a sadistic combing with a flat iron. Yet with self-confidence I pin up my hair, dab fingernail polish on the run in my stocking, rearrange my cleavage, and go on about my business. You see, I have finally decided not to let anything get to me that I have little or no control over. You might call this an epiphany of sorts, or it might simply be my own cockeyed vision for a better quality of life in my golden years.

Women encounter problems that men could never even imagine, beginning at birth, with that first smack on our bottoms. We often experience a loss of identity as we rapidly go from daughter, to sister, to wife, mother, grandmother, great-grandmother and finally, to death. Women suffer from depression, anxiety, boredom and hormones from hell. Some women notice subtle changes in feelings and behavior, while others enter these phases through sudden, dramatic crises.

Bookstores are full of books that give us step-by-step instructions on everything from learning how to turn on your computer to learning how to line dance, with two left feet and pointed-toe boots. So how come there is no how-to guide that describes how you should feel, act and dress when you reach a certain age?

At what age, for example, should you stop wearing skirts up the wazoo and shoes that defy the laws of gravity? Now more than ever, the fashion industry is preoccupied with youth. Everywhere you go, you'll find women trying hard to look like something or someone they are not. (False hair down past their hips, five-inch fingernails painted red, white and blue, green contacts.)

While it is fascinating to see this giddy fashion fanaticism, it's also a little disturbing to see the lengths to which people will go to obliterate their natural selves. True, being yourself without a guidebook takes courage, and finding a happy medium at any age is a challenge.

However, I've found that the secret is to not obsess over mistakes, fashion or otherwise. Women must learn how not to take ourselves so seriously. For example, when I was young, everything mortified me. False fingernail broke off and landed in a date's water glass—mortified. Hair turning a greenish tint after a home dye job—mortified. Today if those things happened, I'd simply take them in stride.

I'm proud to say that few things mortify me today—although I'll admit that discovering that the back of my dress is tucked inside my pantyhose at a party still does.

Baggage Check

One Saturday while on errand duty—picking up dry cleaning, navigating the parking lot of the grocery store and trying not to mow down the looky-loos (you know, people who mosey through the parking lot looking at their fingernails, other men, other women, organizing their coupons to save that 10 cents on tuna)—I saw a bumper sticker that read: "The more I know about men, the more I love my dog."

That sticker haunted me, for it was sad to think that some women are so jaded that they perceive all men as the enemy because of the actions of some. If a pair of your favorite brand of stockings runs before you can even get them out of the package, would you stop buying that brand altogether? Well, some of us might, because we women take the business of our stockings very seriously.

But men and women should not be as disposable as stockings. And if we view people that way, perhaps it's time for some serious baggage checking. No, I am not talking about those handbags we carry that contain everything but the kitchen sink. I am speaking about those thoughts, feelings and behaviors that can be harmful in relationships. I am talking about that negative, emotional residue that remains from every relationship that you have had since being spanked at birth.

For example, some women were raised in households where several generations of women had relationships with physically or emotionally abusive men. These women may have bought into thinking that all men are "dogs." And that old R&B tune that went, "You keep running away from love because the first one let you down," has become their mantra and, sadly, a self-fulfilling prophecy.

We *all* carry some baggage into our relationships. I remember when I was growing up, my mother cautioned me to be circumspect around boys because they only wanted one thing from girls. For a long time, I didn't know what that one thing was, but I was afraid to ask because that might have led to "the talk" again. So, whenever I was around boys, I was careful with everything I had—my chocolate, my chips, my bicycle.

"Yeah, you can ride it, but only to the corner, then you got to give it back." Had I heeded my mother's advice too strenuously, though, I could have been afraid of men all my life.

So how do we check our baggage in relationships? By talking and listening to one another. And that means listening to what is said, not what we want to hear. If you love being one with nature, and the woman you like can't "go" unless the restroom has tile floors, she is probably not the one for you. If you talk long enough, maybe you will find that out. If he has issues with false hair and meat eaters, and you wouldn't be caught dead without your weave and a McRib sandwich, can this spell true love? Such mismatched encounters often result in a heavy load of mistrust, guilt and disappointment.

Like opening a package with a delicate item inside, learning about one another takes time. Of course, couples do continue to date even when it is obvious that the man or woman in question has serious flaws. She thinks, "If I give him a little more time, he may change. He'll stop being so cheap and take me to a real seafood restaurant instead of Captain D's." Meanwhile, he thinks, "Maybe I can get used to her sucking her teeth after every meal. After all, it's only when she eats, and she does diet a lot." But, truth be told, people rarely change. So if your date's habits annoy you on the third date, chances are, they'll still be driving you batty on your 30th visit to Captain D's.

Well-intentioned friends who know little of the issues may encourage you to continue seeing someone who may not be right for you. "Girl, he drives a Navigator, has a Ph.D. and a timeshare," your friends might say. But remember: your friends may carry baggage of their own when it comes to material things. So listen to what they have to say, then make up your own mind. Check your baggage, pray and then prepare yourself to be swept away by love.

Obsessions

My husband says women obsess about everything. Just as I was about to put my hands on my hips and go into my SheNayNay homegirl stance, I realized that he had a point. We do obsess about stuff. We obsess about relationships or the lack thereof. We obsess about our bodies. Are my hips too big? Do these pants make me look fat? Are my ankles too thick? Are my feet too big? Does this dress look cheap? Should I dye my hair, cut my hair, perm my hair? Should I pierce my ears, get a tattoo, go on a diet?

Every sentence we hear is dissected. Man to Woman: "Baby, you sure look good to me today." Woman: "What do you mean today? Didn't I look good yesterday? Yesterday, I wore my Gucci outfit and matching shoes that I spent a month's salary on. Didn't I look good then, didn't I, didn't I?"

Woman to Woman: "Girl, what did you do to yourself? I didn't even recognize you." You wonder what she's trying to say and you analyze her tone of voice. Is it envy, is it sarcastic? Or heaven forbid, sincere?

Every look is scrutinized. She's acting funny toward me. Why is that woman staring at me? Why is he looking at me? Does he want to get with me? He is pretty cute. But he is probably gay or married with children, with a wife who does not understand him and he is just waiting until the kids finish high school to get a divorce. Is he some woman's baby's daddy?

If you are married and don't have children, you probably obsess about that. Do I really want children? Will people think something is wrong with me if the maternal instinct has not bitten me in the butt by now? Do people think I'm selfish because I don't have children?

When we are not obsessing, we are rationalizing. We tell ourselves that life will get better when we meet the right person, get married, have a baby, but right now we are doing OK, thank you very much.

All some of us have to do is look in a mirror to see our worst enemy looking back at us. Our energy is better spent on things that will help us to become healthier, more productive and creative individuals. Some wise person once said we should work like we don't need money, love like we have never been hurt, and dance like no one is watching. I like that advice.

Shopping

H elena was my shopping buddy. This position was not easy to fill, as I had to interview many candidates before I was satisfied that I had made the right choice. Some potential candidates questioned my taste and even my good sense. "You're going to pay that much for those shoes?" one asked. Sometimes, I found myself rationalizing spending my own money. Other times, I would come home without buying anything and fall into bed with a pint of butter pecan ice cream.

Helena and I met at work the day she came in sporting a colorful blouse and skirt set with matching espadrilles, topped by a sassy little straw hat. While other women in our department looked at her with eyes crusted over with envy, I admired her style and recognized that we were kindred spirits. We had many things in common. Both of us had served in the Air Force—among the first women to infiltrate that minefield of testosterone.

And like me, Helena felt that shopping was one of the inalienable rights of women.

Soon, I discovered her uncanny ability to mix and match, thereby creating fabulous outfits. She was the only woman I knew who could pull off wearing a tight black spandex skirt with an orange blouse and Peter Pan collar, and still look like a lady instead of the hoochie one might picture.

Several Saturday mornings found us in her little car careening down the highway toward the stores. Being former soldiers, we always took a minute to plan our strategy. At our favorite shoe store in midtown Atlanta, she would take one side of the room while I took the other, both of us keeping our eyes peeled for bargains for the other. This, we believed, was better than the both of us walking down the same aisle with our tongues hanging out over the wares. Stores have a problem with drool on their goods. Besides, we could cover more ground this way. And if we were lucky, we would have enough time to stop by one of the outlet stores and pick up a couple of discounted outfits. A really good day for us would be a complete outfit or two and several pairs of shoes.

Today the allure of shopping via computer in your bathrobe at midnight may do it for some, but for me nothing can replace shopping with a friend. Observing a girlfriend when she first spots a sign that says "sale" is truly amazing. I've come to know that shopping is a ritual that can cement relationships between women. After all, shopping together sometimes requires you to reveal your personal style and sometimes your old underwear. Yet, like all things, shopping should be done in moderation. You have a problem if overdue credit card bills are wedged alongside your shoe trees in your brand-new shoes.

Helena is now a married, working mother of two living out of state. On the telephone the other day she mentioned coming to Atlanta for a few days. I can't wait. The first thing we will do after we hug and kiss will be to jump in the car and head to our favorite shoe store.

Layaway, the Zen of Waiting

My mother swore by layaway. Heralded as a way to own things over a period of time, layaway used to be big business. All of our back-to-school clothes were laid away at department stores like Sears. Christmas gifts from underwear to bicycles and all items in between were set aside with a down payment and a sworn oath to make regular installments for the next 60 days or so. Easter and birthdays were more than notations on wall calendars—and showers, baby and bridal, kept pocketbooks crammed full with layaway slips.

The wanting of stuff when our money is funny is a fact of life. How many times have we seen an outfit, a pair of shoes or something so fabulous that we just had to have it or we swore we would simply expire right there on the spot? But we couldn't buy it because we didn't even have two nickels to rub together. Back in the day, layaway was the answer.

My friend Helena, a connoisseur of clothing, loved layaway. Many a day found me holding on for dear life as she careened around corners, racing to pay on her bounty. Often, we barely made it before the store closed on the day her payment was due.

The concept of layaway was on my mind as I drove home one afternoon. The radio was on as usual, yet I was only half listening to it. Since I'd forgotten to thaw out anything, my mind was on what I was going to fix for dinner. A commercial caught my attention, though. Perhaps it was because the woman speaking sounded so hyper and cheery when I was feeling just the opposite. "I have been wanting to have some cosmetic surgery done for some time now," the voice on the radio said, "and I just discovered Dr. So and So who will let me make payments over time. I am just so excited, I can't wait."

Hmmmm. Plastic surgery on layaway. Picture it: Fifty dollars this week on your breast implants, $70 next week on your liposuction. But what if you were like Helena, who played layaway roulette, and you forgot one time too many to make a payment on your implants? Would they repossess them? If you failed to pay the balance on your lipo, would they put the fat back? All these questions and more plagued me as I thought about this commercial.

I am not knocking plastic surgery or anyone who desires it. But I would advise thinking things out before going under the knife. Plastic surgery can be expensive. I would hate to turn down nights out with family and friends because I am still paying on body parts. "Girl, I can't go shopping this weekend, I got to pay on my eyes."

Layaway, I decided long ago, is not for me. Like many people, I crave instant gratification. When I make up my mind to buy something I want it then, not 30 or 60 days later. Now I do admit to hiding items behind other stuff until I can come back later and buy it—say, a beautiful painting of roses behind one of dogs playing poker. But I am always mindful of that old saying: you get what you pay for. I suspect this is true whether you are shopping for a new dress or a new nose.

Girls' Night Out

"All thoughts will be joyous. All discussions that are not joyous will be terminated immediately," read the invitation to a Girls' Night Out. What do you get when you combine 14 talented professional women with good food and beautiful surroundings? You get an evening of sisterhood and laughter—life's glad trumpets and singing violins.

Oh what a joyful noise we made. As the champagne flowed, so did the stories that allowed our souls the freedom to sing and dance in wonderful abandon. We were women of varied ages, single, divorced, married, with and without children.

The mellow sounds of Billie Holiday and Nancy Wilson cloaked us in a cozy cocoon of kinship. Coming from a legacy that created a feeling of connectedness and appreciation of things past, the women were eager to share the experiences that kept them grounded and strong. And they did so with pride and with a tinge of vulnerability.

One woman described the special birthday brunch arranged by her spouse on her 40th birthday. Her adoration for her man was so tangible we felt like we could almost reach out and grab hold of it. A young woman born and raised in South Africa passed around a voting ballot and described what it was like for her to vote for the first time just a few short years ago. She spoke of old women who waited patiently in long lines just to enjoy this privilege. As she spoke, I thought of my polling place just up the street from my house. Why, I could walk there in less than five minutes if my body craved exercise instead of peach cobbler. Hearing her speak, I felt ashamed at my own apathy.

As these 14 women shared their hopes and dreams, I realized that this girls' night out was unlike any that I had ever attended. There were no half-naked men gyrating on tables while I fumbled for dollar bills to stuff in their briefs, no frantic women egging the dancers on with their ribald chants. And there were no swaggering men with breath as bad as their opening lines, awaiting "last call" before trying to make a love connection.

This girls' night out provided surroundings that were loving and supportive in a world that has often been alienating. For those whose hearts may have been bleeding, it was a healing environment. And though we came as acquaintances, I'd like to think that at the end of the evening, 14 women left as friends.

Why Do Women Go to the Restroom in Pairs?

Inquiring men want to know the answer to this age-old question. Nothing seems to fascinate a man more than when one woman in a group of diners asks to be excused from the table, and on cue, every woman at the table gets up to accompany her. Talk about clearing a room. This mass exodus leaves men to do a variety of man things—twiddle their thumbs, unbuckle their belts, belch out loud, flirt with the waitress, or make eye contact with a woman dining alone.

What is the mystery behind this ritual? You don't see men going to the restroom together—at least not without the sound a hundred raised eyebrows would make. Men see the long restroom lines at every event, and they wonder why women don't seem bothered by the lines.

After all, these are the same women who plant their hands on their hips and begin patting their high-heel feet if their men are two seconds late picking them up from work, or for some social event. These are the same women who lean on their horns if you do not go before the light turns green if they are on their way to the mall or the beauty salon.

And heaven only knows what these women talk about during their bathroom sojourns. Do they bash men? The food, the restaurant, each other? Oh to be a fly on the wall of the women's restroom, men think. Then they shudder when the reality of that possibility actually dawns on them.

Truth is, there's really no mystery as to why women go to the restroom in pairs or in groups. Ladies just think it's nice to have someone to talk with as they powder their noses and repair their lipstick. Sometimes women need to escape to a place that lets them unwind for a few minutes.

After all, it takes effort to talk intelligently, keep your stomach sucked in and breathe at the same time in a dress that fits like a second skin. And just like men sometimes have to unbutton the waistband of their slacks or scratch themselves and burp, so do women. Only women try to do it in private.

Women may chat about men in general, their dates, their significant others, their children or their jobs. Yet often these restroom excursions simply give them a few minutes alone with friends. In those few minutes, women can share beauty tips, try on a new lipstick, or get an honest opinion on how they look.

Yes, going to the restroom in groups is a woman thing. Like the reason women have so many shoes, men simply wouldn't understand.

A Good Man

Often when a group of women are gathered, the conversation invariably turns to the question of where the good men are. A few years ago, the answer might have been: "In Atlanta." At least that's what some magazines reported. When women read that Atlanta was the land of man candy, suddenly the sound of luggage snapping shut was heard like a shot around the world. And since millions of women read the same articles, you can guess what happened.

Older women used to tell us that churches were good places to find good men. Others declared that art galleries, museums and cultural events were male magnets. Still others suggested that supermarkets were good meeting places, arguing still that the way to a man's heart is through his stomach.

Even with all these meeting-place suggestions, many women are still singing that old Al Green song, "I'm So Tired of Being

Alone." Curious, I asked several women friends what they felt defined a good man. Not surprisingly, financial security topped the list of must-haves, while having his own teeth also was a plus. But many women seem to be attracted to men who are tall in stature but short on character.

It seems to me that the good men we see sweeping the halls of our workplaces, or riding on the backs of dump trucks, are usually not flashy enough or rich enough to turn most women's heads. These women only have eyes for the Denzels and the Tom Cruises of the world, with their bulging pecs and even bulkier wallets. Many somehow mistake an Armani suit and a Lincoln Navigator as symbols of success, breeding and class.

A good man may not remember your birthday or Valentine's Day with chocolates and flowers, but he may change the oil in your car and rotate your tires. This concern for your safety says he loves you as well as any syrupy words could. And for some women, the sweet-nothings and other small tokens of affection are not enough. Even when their partner says all the right things and gives the most thoughtful gifts, they feel cheated that they didn't get something better. Some women don't feel it's really love unless their man buys them a diamond or a Lexus he can't afford.

Some women equate love with what they see on television, but few people are living that fairytale life for real. Only on television do people wake up with breath that is kissing-fresh. Reality is often eye crust and breath screaming for Scope. If they're not careful, some women could miss out on their own fairytale by buying into the myth that only white-collar types with a platinum card and BMW will do.

I am one of the lucky ones—a woman blessed with a good man. And while he may think that putting down the remote control every now and then is actually communicating, he shows his love in many other ways. He soothes me on days when I have bumped my head on the glass ceiling and fought off road rage. And while he may not be good with words, the man is great with his hands. And believe me, those hands speak volumes.

S-e-x

I t should be obvious to even the most unobservant that the world is fixated on sex. Check out the cover of any women's magazine, and titillating titles like "Does size matter?" or "Lights on or off?" grab your attention. And both women and men sometimes find themselves thumbing through page after page of popular magazines in a frenzied search for sexual secrets.

Let's face it. Sex sells. And the sexual revolution has produced a society totally obsessed with it. People are consuming Viagra like cornflakes. Even with the threat of AIDS and other sexually transmitted diseases, some people are still playing Russian roulette by engaging in one-night stands. Erotic messages bombard television, while parents with remote control in hand click away at commercials and oversexed TV shows. And while no African-Americans have ever recalled meeting the Nielsons, we all know that television programming is solely about the ratings and the benjamins (dollars).

And what's a music video without scantily clad males and females engaging in a little bump and grind? These videos are chockfull of graphic words as well as sexual imagery of adultery and infidelity. They portray young people who apparently will do and have done everything, and who are not bothered by the fact that their parents witness their erotic behavior, along with millions of people across the nation. They make Hester Prynne of *The Scarlet Letter* look like Snow White—although Snow living alone in the backwoods with seven men could raise a few eyebrows.

How about today's popular music? A couple of years ago, one popular song declared, "I want to sex you up." That wasn't even grammatically correct. Then we found ourselves popping our fingers to a tune that asked the question, "Where do you want me to put it?" I say if you don't know, then I am not going to tell you. Yet we all knew where the singer wanted to put it, and it wasn't in a sock.

My godson says such lyrics reflect a sort of sexual lingo that a young man must use when he is trying to mack, to seduce a potential partner. It's been more than a quarter of a century since I've dated, so I can't recall if I ever macked. I don't even know whether women can officially mack.

To young people who justify their sexual exploits by declaring that everyone is doing it, I ask: How do you know? Then I tell them that while real men reportedly don't eat quiche, real men and real women keep their business to themselves. Real men and real women respect as well as protect themselves.

Body Beauty

Diets

I have tried them all: the grapefruit diet, the cabbage diet, the fruit diet. I've tried the protein diet, where you eat all the protein you want. For the meat lover in me, this was great, but I soon got tired of chewing. Next I tried a diet that consisted of eating nothing but legumes. I tried pinto beans, navy beans, red beans and black beans. But this diet produced quite a side effect.

Then there was the water diet, where I consumed bathtubs full of water. That, too, had a downside, causing me to spend too much time in the restroom. And at public places where lines for the women's restroom are always long, this was serious. The combination of long lines and the water diet culminated in some new dance steps. Friends expressed surprise that at my age I could still "get jiggy with it," and without music.

Desperate, I even made up diets. One day all I ate was tomatoes. That night I dreamed that a head of lettuce and ranch dressing were stalking me. Another time, all I ate was watermelon. Still another time, it was boiled eggs. That night, for some reason, I felt this strange urge to cluck.

I popped diet pills, drank diet teas and chewed diet gum. But let me warn you: Do not order diet items by mail, for this alerts every diet guru alive that you are dieting. I once received a letter from some doctor in Australia who claimed to know what I was going through. Then, this man told me he had just the diet for me. Next, there was one from Canada and—you guessed it—the Canadians, too, knew what I was going through and had just the diet for me. This diet was made from bee pollen and guaranteed that I could lose 10 pounds overnight while I slept.

The diet bug bit me one day when I glanced at my naked body as I stepped from the shower. My former brick-house figure, I realized, is now a mansion with a carport. And recently I acknowledged the health hazards attributed to obesity: heart trouble, high blood pressure, diabetes and strokes. Yet media images also threaten my self-esteem and my mental health.

Arming myself with the facts about good nutrition and exercise empowers me. And while I would prefer that my breasts not lie on my plate when seated in a restaurant booth, I am thankful that I am disease-free and healthy. And even as I work to nurture good eating and exercise habits, I remember to love the body I have.

Full Figured

Four years ago when I broke my ankle, I joined the sisterhood of full-figured women. Before then I had been sort of a full-figured woman in training, gaining weight and losing it, gaining it back and losing it. Inheriting the fat gene from the maternal side of my family, I knew I was predisposed to this. Once while visiting relatives in the small town where my mother grew up, a stranger approached me in Wal-Mart. "Hey, aren't you one of the Webster girls' daughters?" he asked. I affirmed that I was. "I knew it," the stranger exclaimed. "You look just like those Webster girls—tall, beautiful, with big hips."

When I was younger, older men described me as statuesque, while soulful, young brothers called me a brick house. Once I was called an Amazon, which I thought was pretty cool because I had read that they were beautiful, strong women warriors. According to mythology, though, they bedded men only to continue their species and then got rid of them permanently—as in death—when they finished with them. Talk about your birth control.

The term "full figured" came about several years ago when people finally acknowledged that the average woman wore a size 14 or larger and had breasts that overflowed their cups. Yet women did not have the license to be full figured until a full-figured model was seen strutting down the fashion runway in all her glory and showed that pencil-shaped women did not hold a monopoly on beauty, style and fashion. Few people knew that Marilyn Monroe wore a size 12 or that Barbie was not a real woman. Had Barbie been a real woman, I suspect she would have had difficulty walking upright with her proportions.

While the media has introduced us to some attractive, full-figured high achievers (Oprah Winfrey, Starr Jones, Delta Burke), many of us knew beautiful, large-size women we admired when we were growing up. Sometimes they were our mothers, our aunts or our grandmothers. Often they were our teachers or leaders in our church and community. They exuded beauty and carried themselves with grace in shoes that were size 9 or larger. These women were large and in charge, for they realized that the beauty of a woman is not in the clothes that she wears or the figure that she carries. They understood that beauty is in the soul.

Beauty Shop

For as long as I can remember, my mother did hair. At her shop, the sizzle of straightening combs sliding through greased hair mingled with the arid smells of chemicals used to give black-textured hair a more "permanent" straightening. It was here that blue-haired church ladies dispensed peppermints with Bible verses, and here that I learned about life as a woman.

Women with skin tones ranging from the richest, deepest chocolate to the lightest café au lait (and all shades in between) came to the beauty shop to let their hair down, so to speak. Some of the best storytellers were found at the beauty shop. It was not only a rich source of community gossip, it also was a social club—many friendships were formed in this place where all women were created equal in their quest for beauty. One woman might be getting a shampoo, while another sat under a hot dryer, fast asleep and snoring. There was usually one whose hair was being relaxed, while yet another waited to be hot curled or finger-waved, all with appointments at 11:00.

"What time was your appointment?" one patron might inquire of another. "Mine was 11," one would reply. "So was mine," her neighbor would say, glancing at a wall clock that now glared 11:30. With a sigh, they flipped through outdated Jet magazines, all waiting their turn to be transformed, relishing in this rite of sisterhood.

Reading or playing quietly close by, my sister and I discovered firsthand the secrets of being a woman. Here we picked up tips on everything from lining our lips with an eyeliner pencil before applying our lipstick to ways to keep your man at home where he belonged. For the latter, the methods used varied—from using good sex to "roots." It was not until years later that we enjoyed good sex and learned that "roots" were not what we first imagined.

Only when the stories got really juicy did the women realize that they were suddenly thirsty or hungry and sent us to the store to buy Nehi grape sodas, or RC colas or dinners sold at the neighborhood church to support the usher-board or the church building fund.

At the beauty shop, we learned many things. We learned that the little old ladies with blue hair were not born that way, and that the lady whose hair always looked perfect wore a wig. My sister and

I also learned the importance of uplifting one another as women, and the dignity found in decent, honest work. We learned that being a woman was not always easy. Yet in the faces of each of those women, we saw the memory of the girls we now were—and the beckoning image of the women that someday, if we were lucky, we would become.

Hair

More than just the latest style, a woman's hair is her signature. As a little girl sitting on the floor between loving knees getting our scalps massaged or greased, we learned lessons in living. Mothers and other relatives, storehouses of oral history, told us stories of women who triumphed over hardships. Women like Harriet Tubman, whose underground railroad led our ancestors to freedom. And women like Madam C.J. Walker, who made hair care a mega-buck business, and showed women that they could better themselves and become economically independent.

Like many girls my age, I wore my hair braided so tight that my scalp puckered. I hated my plaits and often longed for a ponytail or something freer. On days that my mother had to go to work early, she would braid my sister's and my hair the night before to save time, and we would wear hairnets to bed to protect our mother's hard work. My sister, being "tender-headed," would flinch if you even looked like you were coming near her with a comb. And forget the hot comb. After a round with this dangerous instrument, my sister's hair looked nice and straight, but her ears often looked like they had been barbecued.

Saturday nights were prime times for this ritual, and while whiffs of bergamot mingled in the air with confidences shared, time seemed to stand still. Perhaps this is why, as we grew into women, Saturday became the most popular day for visiting the beauty shop. Could it be that we were attempting to recreate that special ritual from our childhoods? Perhaps combing our kitchens (the hair at the nape of the neck) was about much more than being groomed. Perhaps it was about being nurtured and lovingly ushered into womanhood.

Full Circle

W hen I was a teenager, I was incensed when my mother wouldn't let me get my ears pierced. The other day, though, I saw a young girl who looked like she had been pierced by somebody on drugs. Her nose was pierced, as was the corner of her lip, and rows of gold studs lined both ears. There was a small loop piercing her eyebrow and when she opened her mouth, I saw a small gold ball in her tongue. She probably even had piercings in some of those unmentionable spots I sometimes hear people mention. The very thought of that makes me cross my legs.

When I was growing up, my Uncle Johnny was the only person I knew who had a tattoo. It was a heart with an arrow separating the two halves. He said he got it on leave during the war. According to him, this was a ritual that soldiers did when they crossed the ocean for the first time. I wondered what they did when they crossed back over.

Used to be if a woman woke up on a bad hair morning, she simply plopped a wig on her head or brushed her misbehaving hair back in a French roll and away she went. Now if you wake up with short hair and show your beautician enough money, by 5 p.m. you can have hair down to your toes. And what we used to call plaits are now called braids, enticing women to spend hundreds of dollars and sit for hours to get a certain style.

Long before I developed my womanly roundness, pedal pushers covered my gangly figure. They were plaid, of course, for back then plaid must have been the affordable fabric, because there seemed to be so much of it. Today, pedal pushers are called Capri pants and once again are all the rage.

"Retro" is the term used to identify items that have come back into use. Mohair sweaters, white lipstick and platform shoes have all returned to favor, and teens everywhere are raiding their mothers' closets looking for clothes to wear to retro parties.

Recently as I watched television, I saw that "The Wizard of Oz" was being repeated for the umpteenth time. I first watched this classic as a little girl, mimicking Dorothy as I clicked my heels in my tennis shoes and exclaimed that there was no place like home. Decades later, Dorothy is as unscathed as ever. How has she made it into the 21st century with those perky braids? To keep up with the times, by now Dorothy might have purple hair, a tattoo or two and something pierced. I did hear, though, that Auntie Em was hosting a talk show in Kansas for people who followed the yellow brick road and couldn't get that song out of their heads.

The women who influenced my life as I was growing up were often 15 or 20 years my senior. They were teachers, beauticians and housekeepers. From them I got a glimpse of who I was and who I hoped to become. Today, I am the mentor, the teacher and the person young people talk to about life, sex and whether they should go out with a guy they just met on the Internet.

And it is up to me to tell them the truth as I see it, and to lead by example. I am constantly in awe of this great responsibility that I have. Yet I accept it gladly, for I realize that I have been blessed to live long enough to see many things come full circle.

From the Outside In

Stockings, the Beginning

You know the story. You buy stockings in your favorite shade and you take them home, put them away in your stocking/ underwear drawer until you are ready to wear them. Then it happens. You are getting dressed to go out. You open up a package, carefully rolling them down like your mother showed you. You maneuver them over your foot, gently pulling them up your leg, all the while sucking in your stomach and holding your breath. You are smoothing them on your thighs when suddenly the fabric catches on your ring and before you can even blink, a run races down your leg like water.

You do one of three things, depending on where the run is. You dab a little clear nail polish on it to stop it from running, or you take off the offending garment and fling it across the room and open up another pair. Or you keep on the pair with the run and feign surprise when someone comments on it.

A pair of stockings is usually the one garment you can get your significant other to buy for you. They usually are the least embarrassing, and the one thing that he will probably not get wrong. All you have to do is tell him the size, the shade and the exact store where you usually buy them.

I remember my very first pair of stockings. It was the Christmas of my 14th year, and these stockings—in a shade called Royal Velvet—were one of the few presents I received that I truly liked. Bought at Sears, they were sheer and black, with a deep purplish tinge that made my long pale legs look halfway good. These stockings were only to be worn on Sundays and for "dress-up," Mama said.

Naturally, she went on to school me about how expensive stockings were and how she could barely afford to buy them for herself. For school, I continued to wear long knee socks or tights of colors that matched my outfits, which, fortunately, was the style at the time.

The first time I wore those stockings, though, I felt totally grown-up. I wore them with a straight knit dress that showed off my budding figure. I remember walking carefully and sitting stiffly so as not to run them. Why, I even bore my sister's teasing in silence; after all, I was now a lady and I was wearing the stockings to prove it.

Girdles

A friend of mine is getting married in a few months and I am starting to panic about what to wear to the wedding. This is a male friend who knew me before my hourglass figure began shifting with the sands of time, before the fat genes took up permanent residence around my hips and thighs.

I have lost a few pounds through diet and exercise, but this process is too slow. And while a Barbie doll physique is not my goal, it is becoming difficult to determine where my breasts end and my stomach begins. So, like many women before me, I have considered buying a girdle to camouflage too much time spent in the company of Ben and Jerry. But where do I start?

I had no idea there were so many styles. You have your body shapers that fall into categories like "moderate" and "moderate control." There are tummy shapers, your all-in-ones, your waist-cinchers and your corset types. Many come in "long-line" styles guaranteeing a firm line from waist to thigh. Many sport a cotton liner and can cost as much as a pair of designer shoes. Then you have your high-cut briefs, although I shy away from anything cut high, since on my hips that immediately translates to thongs—a most unfriendly undergarment, in my opinion.

Even the name brands read like a dieter's dream. Thinner by the Inches, Waist Nippers, and Barely There. If it's barely there, I think, then what's the use? The list goes on. Seductively Slim Briefs, Thank Goodness It Fits, No Body's Perfect, and I Can't Believe It's a Girdle, which to me is too close to that other product's slogan, the one that caused me to need a girdle in the first place.

Once an important part of women's lives, the girdle became passe a few decades ago. But it is now making a comeback. Keeping women fit, trim and unable to breathe continues to be big business. Hanes Intimate Apparel, one of the main sources for girdles and other undergarments, is a subsidiary of Sara Lee, the goddess of baked goods responsible for adding all those pounds. Perhaps a new Sara Lee jingle—"Just wait until you try to put on one of our girdles"—would be enough to make us put down that slice of cheesecake.

As a young girl, I remember helping my mother put on her girdle on a hot summer day. With sweat, talcum powder and our combined strength, we tugged and tugged until my mother emerged as the fine-figured woman men admired. I swore then and there that I would never wear a girdle.

But when that resolution flew out the window and I began looking for one, the first place I checked was the Internet. The girdle sites abound. Girdlebound, Playtex.com, and the Girdle Zone. The Girdle Zone boasts a link called the Girdle Encyclopedia. It can tell you everything but this: Why is it that tummy roll around a woman's waist never disappears, but simply ends up above the waistband of her girdle?

Unfriendly Panties

I f you're like me, you probably grew up with a mother who reminded you to always wear clean underwear just in case you were in an accident—although had I been in an accident, I assure you that dirty panties would have been the last thing on my mind.

Thinking back, it seems that my mother was obsessed with panties. I could always expect two or three pairs for every special occasion. For Christmas, I got candy canes and panties; for my birthday, panties and a birthday cake; at Easter, Easter eggs, a chocolate bunny and panties. In fact, my early introduction to the joys of laundry was washing my panties and socks. Although we had a washing machine, one of those old-fashioned wringer types, I learned to wash my unmentionables by hand.

When I failed to use enough elbow grease on my white socks and panties to please Inspector Mom, she gave me a little scrub board to use. Though it was almost like a toy, it played havoc on my knuckles. Was white the only color for panties back then? Even during my eight weeks of military basic training, I seemed to only own white cotton panties. Did someone decide that colored underwear and combat boots clashed with a nice dirt foxhole?

Having left my mother's house, I felt I was long overdue for some pretty, frilly panties. Upon graduating boot camp, I went overboard with colors, styles and fabrics. I bought panties in pastels, and I bought them in nylon. I bought a pair in black and a pair in red. I bought bikinis, briefs and French cut—just the thing for trips to Paris or to wear while eating French toast. I bought panties embroidered with the days of the week on them. On Monday, I wore my panties that said Monday. On Tuesday, I wore Tuesday panties. Often that was the only way I remembered what day it was. Then I had a thought: What would happen if I wore my Friday panties on, say, Sunday? Unfortunately, that confused me and I think I lost a whole week.

When I got married, however, mixing up my days-of-the-week panties was fun. Wednesdays in our house was deemed hump day for reasons other than it being the middle of the week. So, walking on the wild side, I climbed into my Wednesday panties on a Friday. And, you guessed it, my husband got confused and, voila, hump day again.

Next I tried novelty panties with hearts, moons and stars. Once I bought a pair with a zipper smack dab in the front. They were cute and friendly at first, but when the zipper tried to eat me alive, they had to go. I think this is the first time I ever threw anything out that was still good.

Today in my underwear drawer lie the battle-scarred victims of my various panty experiments. On some the elastic on the waist-band is hanging on by a thread, while others are frayed in the seat. The ones with duct tape are still hanging in there. But lately the ones I wear most often are creeping up on me like a thief in the night, and I find myself looking around to be sure no one is watch-ing while I rearrange them. Meanwhile, I'm slowly accepting the fact that my panties are unfriendly and I need to get some new ones.

I have a lot to choose from, I know. Panties today sport wide, plush-back waistbands for extra softness. Others are pre-shrunk for a perfect fit, while high-cut designs offer another style. At some lingerie stores, panties can cost more than a pair or shoes. At Victoria's Secret, for instance, a sale is three for $25. For me, three pairs for $6.99 will do just fine. My husband says that maybe if I spent more for my panties, perhaps they would last longer. But he's a man who's shopping challenged at best, so what does he know?

Like women who try to cram a size-10 foot into a size-8 shoe, some women, fearing the bloomer syndrome, try to cram their 42-inch hips into size-6 panties. Then there is the full-figured woman in white slacks wearing bikini panties. We know this because we see the outline of her underwear and hear her panties crying, "Help me, help me." And women wonder why their underwear bites back. Ladies, if your size-7 Hanes have started going their own way, you know what you have to do.

I think it was Shakespeare who said, "Life is an endless struggle full of frustrations and challenges, but eventually you find underwear that fits." Or was that my mother?

Bras

I t was a Tuesday when something happened that bothered me all day. It was around 10 o'clock that I realized I had worn the wrong bra. This innocent bit of lace that at first supported my voluptuousness soon became very unfriendly. It developed claws and began digging into my flesh. Then it started to travel upwards, one cup at a time, while one strap slid somewhere around my navel. No attempt at rearranging its contents discreetly worked. Finally at my wits end (or replace the "w" in wits with a "t"), I ran to the restroom to see what I could do, besides ripping it off and going bra-less for the rest of the day. Since my job is not at one of those booty-shaking clubs where not wearing a bra might actually get me more money, this was not an option.

Rumor has it that a man named Otto Titzling created the first bra for women around 1911. OK, these same folks rumored that Thomas Crapper discovered the toilet. Without a doubt, women believe that it must have been a man who invented this torturous

contraption. Truth be known, though, Mary Phelps Jacob was cred-
ited as the inventor of the brassiere that is now widely used. Her
design, however, was not for cups to support the breasts, but to flat-
ten them.

Bras have gone through many innovations. It started with the
training bra, but I skipped that class altogether. Viewing the rav-
ages of time and gravity, it's obvious many women also flunked
this training. And ironically, Madonna got rich by putting on her
blouse before she put on her bra.

One of my first bras was cone-shaped and pointy and looked
like two torpedoes poised to fire. Next came the "cross your heart"
and the "18-hour bra" that I once wore for more than 24 hours on
a trip to the Orient. I wonder if that was some sort of record. Strap-
less bras soon came along to allow women to wear evening clothes
and halter tops. Then came the sports bra or the jogging bra.
Frankly, I might have been tempted to buy one in every color had
they truly been jogging bras that could have gone ahead and jogged
without me.

Today the Wonderbra and the H2O bra have replaced the fiber-
fill-padded bra for the cleavage-challenged. The water bra is pur-
ported to have real water in the cups that mold to a woman's shape
to give that added roundness. And I hear it comes with a freeze
warning for women living in places like the Dakotas and Maine.

Too often, beauty for women is associated with pain. Underwire bras hoist breasts but cut into tender flesh. Bra straps dig into your shoulders and leave dark marks and welts. Girdles have replaced the whalebone corsets of yesteryear that were laced tightly to obtain cleavage and a 10-inch waist. So what if you couldn't breathe without passing out? You looked good the short time you were standing.

And why is it that women can't seem to throw away a bra? Most of us have a drawer full of bras, yet there are only one or two that we wear. Could it be because they are so pretty? Or is it because as girls we coveted them for so long that we see them as badges representing our struggle for womanhood?

Today's bras have come a long way from the black and white cotton designed to support the masses and make mountains out of molehills. But on that fateful Tuesday, had there been women outside my building burning their bras, I would have been leading the pack.

Closet Full of Clothes and Nothing to Wear

I t starts out innocently enough with three little words: "You are invited…" As you glance at the words on that ecru-colored card, a metamorphosis takes place. Your palms tingle, and sweat beads your upper lip. Words like semi-formal, business casual or casual elegance swim before your eyes, and by the time you get to where you must RSVP, you feel lightheaded.

What is casual elegance anyhow? Is it that long black skirt, the one with the thigh-high split that you simply had to have? Would it be casually elegant if you wore it with a white silk blouse? Or maybe you could wear that little black dress with your cultured pearls. Surely you couldn't go wrong with that, could you?

Maybe you had best stay away from black. The last three times you attended an event, you wore black. In fact it started that New Year's eve when that baby-faced, Puff Daddy lookalike asked you to dance. You know, the one who commented that black was a good color for you as it made you look tall and sexy. But repeated questions from women friends asking if you were in mourning made you realize that maybe you had been wearing too much black lately.

That red knit chemise worn with your red high-heel pumps that you bought last month could work. Casually elegant or plain hoochie-mama, you wonder. Nothing quite says vamp—or is that tramp?—like wearing red from head to toe. What about that navy pantsuit with the mandarin collar and frog button loops? Boring and safe, it screams.

In your bedroom, you fling open both closet doors. And like the fashion police, you rifle through the contents, pulling things off hangers and flinging them across the bed, along with the clothes you were wearing. Standing naked in front of a full-length mirror, you stare at your body as you try on various combinations.

Has my butt always looked this big in this black skirt, you wonder. Surely, I haven't gained any weight. Those cleaners have shrunk my skirt. Perhaps the moisture in this house caused this fabric to shrink. Are my breasts starting to sag?
Maybe I need to buy a support bra, maybe in black lace. Darn, this white blouse has a stain on it.

Stopping to exhale, you peek at your checkbook, then at the calendar. And as usual, there is more month left than money. With a less critical eye, you give both the Anne Klein coatdress and the navy pantsuit a second look. Both of these could work. OK, now what about shoes?

Accessories

You've done it. You've shopped until you're ready to drop. Your feet are sore and your ankles look like they belong to elephants. After traipsing from store to store, you finally found the perfect outfit for the occasion. Now the only thing left to think about is how to accessorize.

Dictionaries define an accessory as an object or device not essential in itself, but adding to the beauty and, often, to the value of something. Accessories run the gamut from necklaces to fancy belt buckles. Ankle chains, hats, scarves, pins, rings and watches round out the choices for many spiffy dressers, while some folks argue that tattoos and body piercing should also be included in the accessory category.

When it comes to accessories, however, often good taste and the desire to create a personal statement end up in a visible tug-of-war. Men as well as women sometimes find it hard to decide which of their 14 gold chains they want to wear. So, throwing caution to the wind, they wear all 14 at once. I blame flea markets for this—for making both faux gold and the real thing, while difficult to distinguish, easy to obtain.

We've all seen examples of this before. A fine-looking man walks toward you. There is something about the way he moves, an aura about him that is… well, golden. There is a swagger in his step that says "I know I've got it going on, and you know it too." But as he approaches, you realize that he has O.G.'d—overdosed on gold. That golden smile is the sun glancing off his gold teeth. He is wearing gold on his wrists and on all ten fingers, with a few diamonds thrown in for good measure. And you find yourself running, not walking, before you are struck by lightning or robbed just for standing next to him.

Selecting the right accessory depends on the statement you are trying to make. Does your diamond-encrusted lion pin say, "I am woman, hear me roar?" Or perhaps it says, "I've got it, therefore I must flaunt it."

That dated-looking black suit that has hung in the back of your closet can be easily transformed from tres dull to tres chic, by adding the right hat, pin or scarf. An ornate necklace can become a conversation piece and give you that air of elegance—while dangling doorknob earrings, and wrists laden with bracelets that jingle every time you exhale, are fine if you are Mrs. Santa Claus.

Frankly, individuals who follow their own compass and not society's or some fashion designer's are to be commended. Still the challenge is real. Simply ask yourself: "Girlfriend, do you wish to enhance what you are wearing, or are you trying to stop traffic?" The answer lies in this age-old piece of wisdom: "In all things, moderation is the key."

Purses

The one luxury my mother allowed herself when I was growing up was her pocketbooks. She would spend a couple of hours in a department store trying to find the perfect one. It was usually big, black, had a lot of pockets and was made of leather to last. Thinking back, I don't even know why she bothered being so selective as the real power lay in the small change purse that she kept tucked in her bosom.

I can remember few things more embarrassing than when she would reach into her blouse to get her money. Back in the day, a mugger could have had a real fine time, as he would have had a hard time locating the money. Really, though, a mugger wouldn't have stood a chance with my mom. While her purse may not have carried much money in it, it contained everything else. It had face powder, pictures of us, including our cat, and multiple keys—many without identity, but which could be used as weapons if need be.

Why carry Mace when you had the keys of death?

For many women, as for my mother, their purses are symbols of their action-packed lives. And the purse—and its contents—matures with the woman. Around age three, when a little girl gets her first pocketbook, she might stuff it with a quarter and a hankie for Sunday School and a pair of plastic Barbie shoes. Years ago pre-teen girls carried diaries and pens and lipstick with names like Bubble Gum or Pink Ice. Hankies were replaced by Kleenex used to blot lipstick. A teenage girl's purse today might contain several shades of lipstick with names like Grape or Gothic Midnight. These might co-exist with a comb, tampons and condoms. Computerized organizers have replaced the small autograph book, where friends used to write stuff like "you are one of a kind," or "always stay sexy, crazy, cool." Now teenagers can dial each other on their cell phones.

Today's purses are mood proclaimers. And the styles abound. There are clutches, shoulder bags, backpacks and fanny packs—all in enough fabrics to make your head swoon. Psychologists declare that they can tell more about a woman by glancing in her handbag than they can in two weeks of therapy. As if they'd ever get anywhere near my purse. They can probe my mind, but my pocketbook is off-limits.

In my purse, there is a lot of loose change—a couple of dollars worth—even though I carry a wallet. There are a couple of wadded tissues still good for one more blow. At the very bottom, a corroded cough drop lies naked, having long ago lost its wrapper, and it is courting some fossilized chewing gum. There are tons of ink pens (the reason I have none at work), wadded grocery lists and torn scraps of paper.

During semi-annual cleaning, much of this I throw out. Everything else goes back in: the wallet, two ink pens, my day-planner, a tissue that is wadded but clean. Back they go into my purse, my pocketbook, my traveling security blanket.

Shoes, a Woman's Best Friend

OK, I admit it. I've never met a shoe I didn't like. Put me in a room full of shoes and I become this crazed woman, hands full of footies, pulling boxes off shelves, flinging tissue paper all over, even snatching shoes out of old ladies' hands, while names like Etienne Aigner, Nine West and Proxy dance the macarana in my brain. With my eyes glazing over I try on shoes at stores like Rich's and Nordstrom's, but I am no shoe snob: places like the Shoe Crib and Payless also scream my name.

Nothing gets to me like the smell of leather shoes in the morning, evening or anytime. Open-toe, closed toe, sling-backs, pumps, sandals, western boots, cold-weather boots, this girl loves them all. My passion for shoes started at an early age. When I was a child, my sister and I always had at least three pairs of shoes. We were far from rich, but my mother felt it was important for us to have separate pairs of shoes for the major components of our lives: church, school and play. Church shoes were usually shiny, black patent-leather with straps across the instep with a bow on the toe. At Easter we got its fraternal twin in summer white.

Then we had shoes that we wore only to school. These varied from oxfords made of rawhide suede to black and white saddle shoes. These particular shoes taught me a lesson in patience, as I had to polish them carefully every night before I went to bed, making sure I didn't get any white on the black part.

Play shoes, of course, were only good for play. These might be tennis shoes, school shoes or even church shoes that were no longer fit to wear to those places. If we were caught playing in anything other than our designated play shoes, we got a stern lecture, along with a withering look from our mother.

In addition to these three basic types of shoes, I also wore many whatever-was-on-sale shoes. These were often so ugly that I preferred the threat of bunions later in life. Rather than wear my mother's latest bargain find, I would cram my feet into my old shoes, even if they were too small and cramped my toes.

Shopping for back-to-school or Easter shoes could be either extremely pleasurable or extremely painful. If my mother's pocketbook and fashion sense were in accord, it was great. If they were in flux, you had trouble. Many trips ended with my not getting any shoes, and being led out of the store kicking and screaming.

Historically, shoe tales abound. At Saxon weddings, around 1000 A.D., the father of the bride customarily presented the groom with one of the bride's shoes, symbolizing the transfer of his authority over her. The other shoe was thrown to the bridesmaids, and the woman who caught it was believed to be the next one to marry. Those women who were knocked out by the shoe naturally had to forfeit.

Shoes have been my partners in many struggles. Whenever I am sad, depressed or retaining water, I go out and buy some shoes. Unlike other items of clothing, shoes possess power. They can enhance or ruin an outfit. They also have the power to make us stand proudly and walk tall.

Sandals

I may make some enemies for saying this, but some women should not wear sandals. We have all seen this: A woman is groomed in every way. Every strand of hair is in place, her skin is seemingly smooth to the touch, and she smiles that Colgate smile. Then as our eyes travel downward, there they are: feet that look like they have been barbecued, with crusty-looking hammertoes, and the sides and tops of the feet all plumped out like polish sausages.

On some, the big toes are all balled up, looking like crooked thumbs poised to do Kung Fu with each other. On other women, the big toe is curled up under the rest of the toes. While still on others, the corns on their little toes bulge like pop eyes through the leather straps. Finally there's the woman with the one black toe—the one that was injured yet the nail didn't fall off, but stubbornly stayed on.

Serious corn denial is an affliction with many women. We know this because they strut around with 20 pounds of skin that has yellowed and hardened on their heels. These women would not be caught dead without polish on their toenails, but calluses are A-OK.

Denial about shoe size also abounds. We all know women who will try to cram a size-9 foot into a size-8 sandal—leaving her heels dragging the ground. Or, depending on how the shoe is made, the toes might be leading forward in the mud, forcing the rest of the foot to follow or be left behind.

Finally, there are the women who don't feel they are completely dressed if they're not wearing stockings with their sandals. These are probably the same women who feel naked without a slip. You know who you are.

Today's sandals come in at least two popular styles: the thong and the slide. They run the gamut of styles, including vinyl, rubber, hard plastic in rainbow colors and imported leathers. Some sport stiletto heels, while platforms and flats round out the choices.

Alas, one of our inalienable rights as human beings is the freedom of choice. And I realize that the onset of summer makes you long to wear sandals. But I'd like to offer some advice to my pedicure-challenged sisters: Please remember that imported leather sandals, manicured toenails and hammertoes do not a fashion statement make.

Cool Girls

I was not a cool girl. At last I can finally admit it. School was always a challenge to me. I never mastered math or gym, but English, Spanish and other subjects were a breeze. My most difficult subject was trying to fit in with the "in" crowd. The things that I had going for me—long braids and the ability to pronounce big words—were not qualities to brag about. Invisible is the way I would describe my school years: I was neither a complete nerd nor an egghead, but straddling the middle.

In my high school in Washington, D.C., the cool girls were great dressers. During the 1960s, the shoes to wear were called "Nineteens." Someone said they were called that because they cost $19. They were round-toed, low-heeled, sling-back shoes that came in suede and leather and in colors like navy, black and dark green. The coolest of the cool girls had several pairs in both leather and suede. Cool girls and cool guys wore leather coats.

While the cool students were cool 365 days a year, I on the other hand experienced nanoseconds of coolness. One school year I was allowed to purchase some wool skirts with matching sweaters that were in style. Only crisp white blouses were worn with them. The cool girls wore these matching outfits with their Nineteens and stockings, while I wore mine with matching knee socks and suede oxfords—sort of preppie geek.

For me, achieving even short bursts of coolness required creativity. At school I sometimes swapped clothes with classmates, or changed into forbidden outfits smuggled out of the house in my book bag. I would replace my braids with a cooler ponytail. Peering in the mirror in the girls' bathroom, I lined my eyes with an eye pencil that I "borrowed" from my mother, first licking the tip as I had seen her do many times.

However, when the school bell rang at 2:45, off came the borrowed clothes and the ponytail. Unfortunately, I remembered the eye makeup at the same time my mother noticed it. Silently, I endured her raving-lunatic routine covering various topics: fast girls, keeping up with Joneses (who were those people anyway?) and being yourself. This was followed by the living-under-my roof, eating-my-meat-and-bread, and if-Sally-jumped-in the-lake, would-you-do-it-too sermon.

Today, kids face a whole different set of challenges. With the increased violence in our schools, I shudder to think what the future holds for the non-cool. Childhood, at best, is a time of turmoil and self-discovery. Teenagers crave autonomy from their parents and acceptance from their peers. Yet when you stop to think about it, simply surviving the turbulent school years is, in itself, pretty cool.

Back in the Day

Birth Control

To Betty Lou, wherever you are today, I salute you. You probably don't know this, but you did more for me than birth control could ever do. Because of you, I stoically endured cold showers to cool down the hormonal urges that came along with underarm hair and other bodily changes.

Betty Lou (not her real name) was my high school classmate. Even though we were neighbors, I did not know her or her eight siblings well, but I assumed that she did what I and other girls our age did—primped in the mirror, gossiped about boys and whispered about s-e-x.

The Christmas of my fifteenth birthday, while I got white underwear and books, Betty Lou got a baby: a cute little thing with dimples. Too soon she crossed that line of reading, writing and arithmetic to 2 a.m. feedings, diaper rash and colic. At age 15, the same year the U.S. Supreme Court struck down the one remaining state law (in Connecticut) prohibiting the use of contraceptives,

Betty Lou slid off the short road of girlhood into forever. But who was Betty Lou? Did she, like most girls, harbor secret thoughts of wedding coordinators and bridal registries; of love, marriage and then parenthood? Like her older sisters, Betty Lou was searching for something, maybe someone, to love. And like them the results had been the same. Yet to us girls, Betty Lou took on a new persona. For she had done what many of us had only fantasized about. She had done the deed. Was it sweet like candy, we wondered, or slightly sour like that first bite of dill pickle that locked your jaw and attacked your taste buds, only to mellow out with the next bite and the next?

At neighborhood block parties, Betty Lou was known as a good dancer. Had the rhythm method failed her this time? Or perhaps it was the French kissing that did it. We had heard that you could get pregnant by French kissing. My mother alluded to this during our "talk." But when I asked for clarification, she didn't seem to know much about it. Always fascinated by the exotic, I promised myself that I would research all things French more thoroughly.

All it took was for Betty Lou, with her little baby in tow, to walk by our house to start my mother on her madwoman tirade. "See Betty Lou. That's what you get for being so fast," she ranted. "Just look at her and that cute little baby. And where is the boy?" she asked rhetorically. "They get you pregnant then they leave you holding the bag. If you get pregnant, you cannot stay here, and I mean it…"

To us, Betty Lou became "invisible." We were forbidden to associate with her, for fear that somehow our own virginal chastity would be compromised. We spoke when we saw her, but we could not do anything that could be perceived as if we condoned her behavior. Sure, today unwed motherhood is as common as wearing white shoes in winter, but when I was a girl, it was considered unacceptable behavior.

And while Betty Lou rarely made eye contact, there was something there, a void that ached of a loss not yet definable. And something else, too: a sort of pride that she could make something so pretty, so perfect. Was this why she and the baby took their daily conspicuous walks? Could it have been a warning that we too could someday get caught in this trap despite lectures of proper decorum and abstinence?

Later, as I prepared to graduate from high school with my eye to the future, Betty Lou prepared for the birth of her second child. As I anticipate my 28th wedding anniversary, I think of Betty Lou and wonder where she is today. With compassion born of maturity, I think of all she must have gone through—the snickers, the rude remarks and the name-calling. But because of Betty Lou's self-sacrifice, I held fast to my girlhood dreams. Crossing my legs, I spurned words of love by any guy running a game. With my eyes on the prize, I held out for "until death do us part." So to Betty Lou, wherever you are, thank you.

Mothers

You've probably heard that old adage, "God couldn't be everywhere, so he made mothers." Mother: the very word conjures up a firestorm of memories and emotions. For many of us growing up, she was the one woman who could get on your last nerve—if she even admitted you had nerves. I remember commenting to my mother once that someone I'd had an argument with "got on my nerves." My mother replied, "What nerves? You are too young to have nerves."

This is the same woman who looked me in the eye once and declared that a laxative would fix all that ailed me. "Mama, I have a headache, acne, I stubbed my toe." "All right, go get me the castor oil," she'd say. Mother, who used her black eye pencil down to a nub and still couldn't bring herself to throw it or anything else away.

Mothers are important to our lives, and we carry so much of our mothers within us. She often is the woman from whom you receive your big hips, your hair, your musical talents or your lack thereof. Sometimes, we blame our mothers for everything wrong in our lives. For example, some of us have convinced ourselves that the reason we can't maintain a relationship is because our mothers bottle-fed us instead of nursed us, or that our anal retentiveness is due to some potty-training trauma.

Take my mother, for example. She was a strong woman, a hard-working, self-made businesswoman. She was a woman ahead of her time, who did not believe in sparing the rod or spoiling her children. She never practiced timeout unless you counted the minutes it took for you to fetch her belt or break off a switch.

From my mother I learned many things. I learned that one fried chicken could feed a family of five, plus company. I learned to pray for what I wanted. Lord, give me strength, she'd say. Or another common prayer: Lord, please don't let me hurt this child.

I also learned that I could be anything I wanted to be—although my response to that was to challenge her and the world around me. Throughout my teen years, my mother and I were constantly at odds over everything, and a kind of permanent tension blanketed us until I ran away from home to join the military.

I hated her strict rules: no pierced ears until I was old enough to pay for them myself. And only sailors, bikers and people of that ilk visited tattoo parlors, according to my mother. No makeup until I was 16 and definitely no mini-skirts.

Today, I find myself staring in awe at the mini-skirted young woman in the platform shoes, her midriff bare to show off her newly pierced navel. I gawk at the young man with the pierced tongue and the orange Mohawk, wondering what in the world was he thinking or smoking? Then, to my complete surprise and chagrin, I hear my mother's sayings spring from my lips. It is then that I realize my worse childhood fear has come true: I have turned into my mother.

Sometimes I Feel Like a Motherless Child

Recently a friend shared something that caught me by surprise. It was the anniversary of her mother's death, and she didn't want to spend it alone. In a quiet voice she told me that when she was little, she sometimes felt that her mother hated her. After telling me this she looked at me, trying to gauge my reaction. What she couldn't know was that she had put into words feelings that I could never bring myself to say out loud, and that I felt her pain deep down in my soul.

The mother-daughter bond—that secret society connected through blood and the pain of labor that, according to my mother, lasted for three weeks—does not come with a secret handshake, but with a test of wills. The mother-daughter relationship often comes down to survival of the fittest, as strong-willed women and their stubborn daughters battle over every imaginable issue, from boys to makeup to more serious things.

"I could never do anything right in my mother's eyes," my friend whispered. "Her way was the only way. Hers was always better, quicker, easier, and her constant criticism paralyzed me and I became even more clumsy around her." Boy, could I relate to that. For no matter how others praise you, no opinion matters or makes you more vulnerable than that of your mother.

I wanted to tell my friend how her feelings mirrored my own, but I did not dare interrupt because I knew how difficult it was for her to say things that I suspect she'd never told another soul. How could I tell her that I too had searched for approval in everything I did, every decision I made, yet rarely was it forthcoming? Or when it came, it came with some kind of barb: "You did OK, but next time . . . "

Few of us, I suspect, actually had mothers like Carol Brady of "The Brady Bunch" or Claire Huxtable of "The Cosby Show." I have memories of my mother coming home dead tired from standing on her feet all day doing other people's hair. Yet she still had to wash the hair of two little girls who flinched every time the comb snagged a tight curl. Most days, she was much too tired to listen to our tales of childhood angst.

I remember her middle-age rigidity on everything from miniskirts to pierced ears. And I remember her look of fear the morning when I, at age 14, climbed out of bed and immediately threw up on her bedroom slippers. I also remember the look of relief that swept across her face when the doctor proclaimed it was only the flu.

I have other memories too. I can still see her in the kitchen, an apron tied around her waist, as she peeled an entire apple in one dangling peel for the Sunday cobbler. Out of my father's earshot, I tried to talk to her about the new hair that had sprung up under my arms and "down there." I was concerned that other places might spring hair, too—say like under my chin or the bottom of my feet. I still remember her telling me not to worry about what was going on "down there" in a voice that halted any more conversation. So I never again discussed my changing body or other feelings with her.

Perhaps battling fatigue and wrestling with her own demons, she failed to realize that youth is both fragile as well as fleeting. In hindsight, I can see this now. But at the time, I had no understanding of what a toll it took on my mother to try to be everything for everybody.

One time, I braved punishment and confronted her with questions that had haunted me for years: Why was she always so mean? Why couldn't she be like my friend Denise's mother? I still recall what she said. "The world is not always going to be kind to you, so you had better get used to it now." Then she added: "If you don't like it here, feel free to go live at Denise's house." Of course, I didn't say what I longed to say; I had tempted fate enough for one day. What I wanted to say was that she was not the world, that she was my mother. That for once, I wanted her to listen to me, not try to fix things, not judge me. Was that too much to ask?

Yet with adversity often comes strength. Where nurturing was absent for me, I am now Mother Earth. True to my birth sign, Aquarius, I embrace the world, people, cats, even squirrels.

I also embrace my mother—even though she is long gone. Sometimes when it is quiet, I imagine that I hear her whisper in death words that she seemed never able to utter in life: "You have turned into an amazing woman, my daughter. I always knew that some day you would." For me, the answer is always the same. "Thank you, Mama. I love you."

Waste Not, Want Not

Spoon-fed to me along with my oatmeal was my mother's 11th commandment: "Waste not, want not." I believe it was while I was eating oatmeal for breakfast one morning, yet again, that I first heard it. I had asked for frosted flakes. "Be thankful you've got oatmeal; there are boys and girls in foreign countries who are starving," my mother said. With waste not, want not as my mantra, is it any wonder I can't bring myself to throw anything away?

Born of Depression-era parents, nothing was wasted in our house. If you put food on your plate, you ate it. End of subject. Leftovers were wrapped up and eaten at another meal. Day-old bread was used for a delicious bread pudding. Day-old rice became rice pudding. You took some bologna, onions and spices and you had bologna etouffe.

Everything we owned lived many lives. Washcloths and towels no longer fit to bathe with were used as rags to clean up around the house. Old cotton panties and undershirts were torn up to use as dust cloths to polish furniture and to shine shoes.

In fact, my first sanitary pad was made from a piece of cotton undershirt folded over several times. On the fateful day that my period started, my mother was at work. On the telephone, she walked me through what I should do to tide me over until she could stop by the store on the way home. Somehow, wearing a small pillow between my legs was not what I expected becoming a woman would be like. But I digress.

No items of clothing escaped my mother's penchant for recycling. Old dresses were stripped of their buttons and cut up to use as patches on jackets and jeans. Those discarded buttons and zippers replaced those lost or broken on other garments. Children's clothes that were outgrown by one were passed down to others. If you ran out of siblings to pass things down to and the clothes were still wearable, you passed them down to cousins and other relatives. Old clothes were even cut down and used for doll clothes.

In the kitchen, old cooking pots were plugged up when they sprung a leak and continued in their service. Small jars scraped clean of jelly were washed and used as drinking glasses. The small ones were for juice, and the larger ones were bought piece by piece to make a complete glassware set. Jars not used for drinking would be used for food storage if the lids were intact, while still others were used for canning fruits and vegetables.

Ingrained in childhood, this habit of chronic recycling lives on in me today. I hold on to plastic lids, bottles, ribbons and other items because, I tell myself, you never know when you might need them. I have even thrown things in the trash and taken them back out. Clothes meant for Goodwill often end up piece by piece back in my closet. If I lose about 15 pounds, those straight-leg jeans just might fit. And who knows? Bell-bottom, plaid Capri pants could come back in style.

Vaseline

W hen I was growing up, my mother swore by Vaseline, and our house was never, ever without it. While she sometimes bought hand lotion, the economy-size Vaseline always ruled. This colorless petroleum jelly was used to smooth rough, dry skin all over our bodies from head to toe.

Fighting that uniquely black affliction—ash—African-American mothers often smeared a tiny bit of Vaseline on the faces of little boys and girls. The uses for Vaseline were endless: In our neighborhood, you would see girls on their way to school and church, little bony knees slick and glistening from Vaseline. If they wore patent-leather shoes, chances were their mothers had smeared a little Vaseline on them as well, buffing them with a soft cloth to make them shine. In our house, this same ritual was used to revive all things patent leather—from pocketbooks to belts.

Vaseline was often used to oil little scalps before hair was braided into cornrows and other hairstyles. And it was used on lips to keep them from chapping in cold weather. (Chapstick was something used by people only on television.) While Vaseline was not recommended for burns or wounds, my mother combined this humble jelly with sulfur powder and used the homemade mixture as a salve for burns, rashes and assorted bruises. This remedy was used on pets and humans alike in our house, as Vaseline was revered second only to castor oil—another cure-all for mothers everywhere.

As we girls grew older, we discovered that Vaseline was an excellent beauty aid. We used it to smooth down unruly eyebrows and to darken eyelashes. A dab in your hand mixed with a drop or two of your favorite perfume created scented body oil that lasted all day. Mix a dab with a colored lip pencil, and voila, you had an inexpensive lip-gloss. Why, even supermodels have been known to rub a bit of Vaseline over their teeth to give them that added gleam during photo shoots.

While I am older—and, I hope, more sophisticated—I am still ashy. To combat this dry-skin disorder, I have tried everything from cocoa butter to baby oil. The latter does little for the ash, but it always leaves me smelling baby sweet. I have tried the lotions suggested by friends and enemies alike; still, the ash lives on. And finally when my dry skin starts to crack and bleed, I hear my mother's voice in my head, saying, "Child, put down that lotion and go get yourself some Vaseline."

Comfort Food

W hile I have indulged in the fusion confusion of restaurants that blend different foods like pan-fried tofu tossed on a bed of wild geranium stalks, and dined on dim sum and an assortment of blackened meats, nothing compares to the foods I enjoyed as a girl.

When I was growing up, Sunday-morning breakfasts, always a prelude to Sunday School, consisted of salmon and grits, homemade biscuits (not the kind that pop out of a can) and Karo syrup. Karo, the granddaddy of all syrup, was made of pure cane sugar that dared you to sop it.

And nothing quelled hunger like a bologna sandwich. In my youth, this lunchmeat came in a thick roll protected by a thin skin. It was a deep red color, and you could slice it as thick or as thin as you liked. Slap some mayonnaise on some white bread, pour yourself a glass of red Kool-Aid, and you had a feast fit for a Nubian prince or princess.

Like its first cousin, Spam, bologna was delicious fried. And if you didn't have meat, you could always eat a mayonnaise sandwich.

Chicken—fondly called "the gospel bird" because it often graced the Sunday dinner table—was seasoned, battered and deep fried in lard in a heavy cast-iron skillet to crispy, golden perfection. Or it might be smothered in a rich, artery-clogging gravy or perhaps simmered with flour dumplings in a succulent broth. My mother's yard bird was so good it made you want to haul off and slap the Colonel for half-stepping in the chicken business.

Holiday meals might consist of ham, turkey, neck-bones smothered in barbecue sauce, chitterlings or roast beef. Side dishes might be fried okra, fried green tomatoes, butter beans, string beans, cabbage and collards. Potato salad, macaroni salad, macaroni and cheese and cornbread were also favorites in my house. Golden pound cakes made from scratch with real butter, sweet potato pie, rice pudding, bread pudding with raisins, and peach cobbler usually rounded out the meal. We loved the simplicity of these foods. And, tossing our antacids aside, we feasted with wild abandon, enjoying not just the food but also the family and the fellowship.

I have other fond food memories from my childhood, like sitting at Woolworth's lunch counter eating the best hot dogs that ever twirled round and round on a rack. I also loved White Castle hamburgers, their tiny buns all steamy and soft, and fat dill pickles from a jar.

The hazy days of summer would find my sister and me, pails slung over our arms like silver pocketbooks, going off to pick blackberries for cobbler, and pears and peaches for preserves. Standing underneath a tree loaded with fruit, we swatted at the bees that swarmed around us, realizing that picking the fruit was simply the first step.

Step two found us up to our armpits in fruit peelings, sweltering from the steam of simmering fruit and sterilized canning jars. With sweat stinging our eyes, we embarked on step three: the bonding of three generations of women in the ancient art of preparing food for loved ones.

Whenever I am hounded by a bit of insecurity, I trot into my kitchen and whip up something from my childhood, something traditional that I learned at my mother's side. And as it cooks, I am transported back to another time. As the familiar aromas waft through my kitchen, no matter what is troubling me, a little voice from somewhere deep inside tells me that everything is going to be just fine.

Quick Order Form

Fax Order   404-243-7592

Telephone Order   404-212-9303

E-Mail Order   Inrlight@bellsouth.net

Website Order   www.innerlightpublishing.com

Postal Order   P.O. Box 57143, Atlanta, GA 30343

Please send me copies of :
Venus Chronicles: Musings From the Feminine Side

Price: $12.95

Number of copies: _____

Please send your information for our mailing list:

Name_____

Address_____

City_____State_____Zip_____

Telephone (_____)_____

E-Mail Address _____

Sales Tax: *Please add $3.25 to all orders.*

Payment: ❑ Check   ❑ Credit Card

❑   VISA°   ❑   MasterCard   ❑   DISCOVER

Card Number_____

Name on Card_____Exp. Date ____/____/____

Cardholder's Signature _____